JIM
CODE

CHAMP

JIM CODE

A Glossary of Technological Injustice

By

Champion Muthle

DEDICATION

For my unborn children.

ACKNOWLEDGMENTS

I'd like to thank all the Researchers and Writers who have contributed terms, ideas, and definitions to this glossary, as well as the Activists and Investigators who have lived through these experiences.
Thank you.

INTRODUCTION

There is a new vocabulary of injustice and inequality emerging out of society's advances in technology. We are finding evermore deadly and despicable ways of persecuting and violating the rights of citizens based on race, identity, and social bias. For some, the experiences of these injustices are commonplace; for others, they are completely foreign. Between 2006 and 2014, United States Law Enforcement Agencies underwent a shift towards militarization that paled in comparison even to that which occurred during the 1960s and '70s. This shift created a divide between activists and protestors on the ground and those watching from the safety of their televisions and computer screens, one which continues to this day. The Arab Spring, Occupy Wall Street and the Ferguson Unrest marked the pinnacle of this paradigm shift. The trauma and chaos of this bipolarity has left an enduring scar and social psychosis on the sociocultural framework of America and many other countries around the world. As long as we remain ignorant of these practices, we will continue to fail to find viable solutions and policy changes for them. Hence the need for a new glossary of technological injustice and inequality. This book is just a handful of terms and technologies that exist; it is by no means comprehensive or all inclusive. So long as the militarization of the police and other authorities continues, there will be more, increasingly deadly and devastating, terms and technologies to add.

Sincerely,

Champion Muthle aka Daniel Maree

New York City, New York

December 28th, 2020

ABLEISM

Prejudiced thoughts and discriminatory actions based on differences in physical, mental and/or emotional ability; usually that of able-bodied/minded persons against people with illness, disabilities or less developed skills.

2

ACCESSIBILITY

2

The extent to which a facility is readily approachable and usable by individuals with disabilities, particularly such areas as the residence halls, classrooms, and public areas.

3

ACCULTURATION

3

The general phenomenon of persons learning the nuances of or being initiated into a culture. It may also carry a negative connotation when referring to the attempt by dominant cultural groups to acculturate members of other cultural groups into the dominant culture in an assimilation fashion.

4

ACOUSTIC & NO-TOUCH TORTURE

The use of acoustics, distractor noises, speech processing, and conversational AI to harass, torture, and incapacitate victims of discrimination and police or community targeting. The Voices Obscured in Complex Environmental Settings (VOiCES) corpus is a collaboration between Lab41 (a division of In-Q-Tel) and SRI International. Acoustic torture has been identified as one of the leading causes of Havana Syndrome and is currently being used against American citizens across the United States (including the author).

5

ACTIVE DENIAL SYSTEM

5

An Active Denial System is a non-lethal, directed-energy weapon developed by the U.S. military, designed for area denial, perimeter security, and crowd control. Informally, the weapon is also called the heat ray since it works by heating the surface of targets, such as the skin of targeted human beings. Many activists have also reported having electronic active denial systems running against them in the workplace and at home.

8

ALLY

Describes someone who supports a group other than one's own (in terms of racial identity, gender, faith identity, sexual orientation, etc.) Allies acknowledge disadvantage and oppression of other groups than their own; take risks and supportive action on their behalf; commit to reducing their own complicity or collusion in oppression of those groups and invest in strengthening their own knowledge and awareness of oppression.

9

ANTI-SEMITISM

9

The fear or hatred of Jews, Judaism and related symbols.

10

ARTIFICIAL ANGER & EMOTION

Artificial Anger or Emotion is a tactic used to target and manipulate individuals by faking, confabulating, or generating false responses and information. Artificial Anger is a political tool similar to a wedge issue, which distracts from the true facts and reality of a situation or person for political, economic, or personal gain. Social Media, bots, AI, and fake news are common tools used in the production of Artificial Anger or Emotion.

11

AUTOMATED INEQUALITY & EXCLUSION

Data-based discrimination that affects civil and human rights and economic equity. In her book, Automated Inequality, Virginia Eubanks defines it as the process by which data mining, algorithms, and predictive risk models are systematically used to discriminate against racial and minority groups, and poor and working-class people.

12

BACK & FORTHING / LOOPING / ZIG ZAGGING

Back and Forthing, Looping, or Zig Zagging is a form of emotional abuse, manipulation, and harassment wherein a victim is made to repeat things over and over again ad nauseam. A victim is often pushed in one direction and then in another direction endlessly, hence the phrase zig zagging. The objective is often to slow someone down, infuriate them so that they make a mistake, cause them mental anguish, or make them give up on something that no longer seems achievable or desirable because of the barriers of back and forthing. There are now technological ways to loop people's lives endlessly.

13

BIAS INCIDENT

A discriminatory or hurtful act that appears to be motivated or is perceived by the victim to be motivated all or in part by race, ethnicity, color, religion, age, national origin, sex, disability, gender identity or sexual orientation. To be considered an incident, the act is not required to be a crime under any federal, state or local statutes.

14

BRAVE SPACE

Honors and invites full engagement from folks who are vulnerable while also setting the expectation that there could be an oppressive moment that the facilitator and allies have a responsibility to address.

15

BROKEN BUTTON POLITICS

Broken Button Politics is a phrase coined by the author to describe the systematic disenfranchisement of individuals or groups through the use of technology and poor infrastructure. As government services move online, the ability to block, cheat, or disenfranchise people through technology, whether advertently or inadvertently, has increased significantly. For example, someone who attempts to sign up for a government service with the DMV, Federal Healthcare, or Housing Authority but encounters a series of broken buttons, platforms, or processes is the victim of Broken Button Politics. Politicians often hide behind technology and maintain plausible deniability because the system is made to seem equally available and accessible to everyone when in reality it is not.

16

CANCEL CULTURE

Cancel culture is a modern form of ostracism in which someone is thrust out of social or professional circles online, on social media, in the real world, or both. Those who are subject to this ostracism are said to be "canceled." Although often viewed as an innocent social game, cancel culture can often result in violence and physical abuse for the victims. Many Civil Rights Leaders and Public Intellectuals have spoken out against Cancel Culture. For example, in an interview with Al Jazeera, Dr. Cornel West states, "I'm not on automatic...It's not about identity, it's about solidarity...I don't believe in canceling anybody...You can be obsessed with 'wokeness' and suffer from insomnia...I'm talking about being fortified. That's my tradition."

17

THE CAREN ACT

The "CAREN Act" (Caution Against Racially Exploitative Non-Emergencies) is an ordinance that makes it illegal to make discriminatory, racially biased 911 calls in San Francisco. Similar to California's AB-1550, the Discriminatory Emergency Calls Law, the CAREN Act was introduced in July 2020. The ordinance's name is a twist on "Karen," the name social media gives people making racially biased 911 calls.

18

CATEGORIZATION

The natural cognitive process of grouping and labeling people, things, etc. based on their similarities. Categorization becomes problematic when the groupings become oversimplified and rigid (e.g. stereotypes).

19

CIS-GENDER

19

A person who identifies as the gender they were assigned at birth.

20

CLASSISM

Prejudiced thoughts and discriminatory actions based on difference in socio-economic status, income, class; usually by upper classes against lower classes.

21

CO-OPTATION

21

Various processes by which members of the dominant cultures or groups assimilate members of target groups, reward them, and hold them up as models for other members of the target groups. Tokenism is a form of co-optation.

22

COLLUSION

When people act to perpetuate oppression or prevent others from working to eliminate oppression.

COLONIZATION

23

Colonization, or colonisation is the establishing of colonies. In the case of settler colonialism large-scale population movements take place where the migrants maintain strong links with their or their ancestors' former country, gaining significant privileges over other inhabitants of the territory by such links.

24

COLOR BLIND

The belief in treating everyone "equally" by treating everyone the same; based on the presumption that differences are, by definition, bad or problematic and therefore best ignored (i.e., "I don't see race, gender, etc.").

25

CONSCIOUS BIAS (EXPLICIT BIAS)

25

Refers to the attitudes and beliefs we have about a person or group on a conscious level. Much of the time, these biases and their expression arise as the direct result of a perceived threat. When people feel threatened, they are more likely to draw group boundaries to distinguish themselves from others.

26

CRITICAL RACE THEORY

Critical race theory in education challenges the dominant discourse on race and racism as they relate to education by examining how educational theory, policy, and practice are used to subordinate certain racial and ethnic groups. There are at least five themes that form the basic perspectives, research methods, and pedagogy of critical race theory in education:

- The centrality and intersectionality of race and racism

- The challenge to dominant ideology

- The commitment to social justice

- The centrality of experiential knowledge

- The interdisciplinary perspective

27

CULTURAL APPROPRIATION

The adoption or theft of icons, rituals, aesthetic standards, and behavior from one culture or subculture by another. It is generally applied when the subject culture is a minority culture or somehow subordinate in social, political, economic, or military status to appropriating culture. This "appropriation" often occurs without any real understanding of why the original culture took part in these activities, often converting culturally significant artifacts, practices, and beliefs into "meaningless" pop-culture or giving them a significance that is completely different/less nuanced than they would originally have had.

~

28

CULTURAL REPRESENTATIONS

Cultural representations refer to popular stereotypes, images, frames and narratives that are socialized and reinforced by media, language and other forms of mass communication and "common sense." Cultural representations can be positive or negative, but from the perspective of the dismantling structural racism analysis, too often cultural representations depict people of color in ways that are dehumanizing, perpetuate inaccurate stereotypes, and have the overall effect of allowing unfair treatment within the society as a whole to seem fair, or 'natural.'

CULTURALLY RESPONSIVE PEDAGOGY

Culturally responsive pedagogy facilitates and supports the achievement of all students. In a culturally responsive classroom, reflective teaching and learning occur in a culturally supported, learner-centered context, whereby the strengths students bring to school are identified, nurtured and utilized to promote student achievement.

30

DATA COLONIALISM

31

Introduced by Nick Couldry and Ulysses A. Mejias in **The Costs of Connection**, Data Colonialism is the normalization of the exploitation of human beings through data, just as historic colonialism appropriated territory and resources and ruled subjects for profit. Data colonialism paves the way for a new stage of capitalism driven by human data.

31

DEEPFAKES & DOUBLE DEEPFAKES

Deepfakes and Double Deepfakes are synthetic media in which a person in an existing image or video is replaced with someone else's likeness or voice. Deepfakes leverage powerful techniques from machine learning and artificial intelligence to manipulate or generate visual and audio content with a high potential to deceive.

DEGREE DENIALISM

In the psychology of human behavior, denialism is a person's choice to deny reality as a way to avoid a psychologically uncomfortable truth. Denialism is an irrational action that withholds the validation of a historical experience or events when a person refuses to accept an empirically verifiable reality. Degree Denialism is a form of denialism whereby individuals deny the academic and professional accomplishments and expertise of an individual in order to block their progress and deny or withhold services. Degree Denialism is similar to Citizenship Denialism whereby individuals erroneously question and deny the birth and citizenship of certain individuals, such as what occurred with President Obama.

33

DIALOGUE

Communication that creates and recreates multiple understandings (Wink, 1997); it is bidirectional, not zero-sum and may or may not end in agreement. Dialogue can be emotional and uncomfortable, but is safe, respectful and has greater understanding as its goal.

34

DISCRIMINATORY DESIGN

35

Deepfakes and Double Deepfakes are synthetic media in which a person in an existing image or video is replaced with someone else's likeness or voice. Deepfakes leverage powerful techniques from machine learning and artificial intelligence to manipulate or generate visual and audio content with a high potential to deceive.

35

DIVERSITY

The wide variety of shared and different personal and group characteristics among human beings.

36

DOMINANT CULTURE

37

The cultural values, beliefs and practices that are assumed to

be the norm and are most influential within a given society.

ELECTRONIC HARASSMENT

Electronic harassment is the use of electronic torture techniques to harass, torture, and manipulate the minds and bodies of targeted individuals, predominantly activists and protesters. It includes the use of directed energy weapons (DEWs), electromagnetic radiation (such as the microwave auditory effect), radar, and surveillance technology to transmit sounds and thoughts into people's heads, affect people's bodies, and harass people.

EAVESDROPPING

Eavesdropping is the act of secretly or stealthily listening to the private conversation or communications of others without their consent in order to gather information. The practice is widely regarded as unethical, and in many jurisdictions is illegal. Many activists report being spied on and illegally wiretapped by authorities and political opponents. New, incognito forms of wiretapping via radiofrequency or microwave weapons, such as the kind that occurred against American Diplomats in Cuba, are known to cause actual physical and psychological harm to the victims. There is often little or no recourse against culprits for this kind of abuse; however, states such as Rhode Island have begun implementing new laws to help protect citizens and prosecute culprits.

39

EQUITY

Takes into consideration the fact that the social identifiers (race, gender, socioeconomic status, etc.) do, in fact, affect equality. In an equitable environment, an individual or a group would be given what was needed to give them equal advantage. This would not necessarily be equal to what others were receiving. It could be more or different. Equity is an ideal and a goal, not a process. It ensures that everyone has the resources they need to succeed.

EURO-CENTRIC

41

The inclination to consider European culture as normative. While the term does not imply an attitude of superiority (since all cultural groups have the initial right to understand their own culture as normative), most use the term with a clear awareness of the historic oppressiveness of Eurocentric tendencies in U.S and European society.

41

FMRI FEEDBACK LOOP & NEGATIVE BCI

Functional magnetic resonance imaging or functional MRI measures brain activity by detecting changes associated with blood flow. This technique relies on the fact that cerebral blood flow and neuronal activation are coupled. When an area of the brain is in use, blood flow to that region also increases. fMRI is a type of Brain-Computer Interface (BCI) that can be weaponized, manipulated, turned against individuals, and used without their knowledge or consent. Many scientists and activists have called for Moral, Ethical, and Legal guidelines for the use of this technology, which has the power to violate the Freedom of Thought and Mental Integrity of the people.

42

FRONTLOADING

Frontloading is the biased process of undercutting, ruling out, misjudging, or undermining someone's value, potential, or dignity based on stereotypes. Frontloading is a common practice in job interviews and HR. For example, an interviewer may reify social biases by adding additional layers to an interview before objectively deciding the candidate's suitability for the role. Rather than waiting until the end of the interview to decide the next steps, the culprit would, at the outset of the conversation, state that the candidate will be required to have additional interviews before a decision can be made. Meanwhile, a candidate that fits the culprit's worldview would not be made to do additional interviews.

FUNDAMENTAL ATTRIBUTION ERROR

A common cognitive action in which one attributes their own success and positive actions to their own innate characteristics ('I'm a good person') and failure to external influences ('I lost it in the sun'), while attributing others' success to external influences ('He had help and got lucky') and failure to others' innate characteristics ('They're bad people'). This operates on group levels as well, with the in-group giving itself favorable attributions, while giving the out-group unfavorable attributions, as a way of maintaining a feeling of superiority, i.e. "double standard."

44

GANGSTALKING

45

Gangstalking is the perceived or actual stalking and targeting of individuals by other individuals, groups or communities. It denotes a pattern of repeated, unwanted intrusion by groups or gangs into the life of another in a manner that causes distress, disruption, or fear.

45

HATE CRIME

46

Hate crime legislation often defines a hate crime as a crime motivated by the actual or perceived race, color, religion, national origin, ethnicity, gender, disability or sexual orientation of any person.

46

HETEROSIXISM

47

Viewing the world only in heterosexual terms, thus

denigrating other sexual orientations.

IMPOSTER SYNDROME

Refers to individuals' feelings of not being as capable or adequate as others. Common symptoms of the impostor phenomenon include feelings of phoniness, self-doubt, and inability to take credit for one's accomplishments. The literature has shown that such impostor feelings influence a person's self-esteem, professional goal-directed-ness, locus of control, mood, and relationships with others.

48

INCLUSION

49

Authentically bringing traditionally excluded individuals and/or groups into processes, activities, and decision/policy making in a way that shares power.

INCLUSIVE LANGUAGE

Refers to non-sexist language or language that "includes" all persons in its references. For example, "a writer needs to proofread his work" excludes females due to the masculine reference of the pronoun. Likewise, "a nurse must disinfect her hands" is exclusive of males and stereotypes nurses as females.

INSTITUTIONAL RACISM

51

Institutional racism refers to the policies and practices within and across institutions that, intentionally or not, produce outcomes that chronically favor, or put a racial group at a disadvantage. Poignant examples of institutional racism can be found in school disciplinary policies in which students of color are punished at much higher rates that their white counterparts, in the criminal justice system, and within many employment sectors in which day-to-day operations, as well as hiring and firing practices can significantly disadvantage workers of color.

INTERCULTURAL COMPETENCY

A process of learning about and becoming allies with people from other cultures, thereby broadening our own understanding and ability to participate in a multicultural process. The key element to becoming more culturally competent is respect for the ways that others live in and organize the world and an openness to learn from them.

INTERSECTIONALITY

An approach largely advanced by women of color, arguing that classifications such as gender, race, class, and others cannot be examined in isolation from one another; they interact and intersect in individuals' lives, in society, in social systems, and are mutually constitutive. Exposing [one's] multiple identities can help clarify the ways in which a person can simultaneously experience privilege and oppression. For example, a Black woman in America does not experience gender inequalities in exactly the same way as a white woman, nor racial oppression identical to that experienced by a Black man. Each race and gender intersection produces a qualitatively distinct life.

IN-GROUP BIAS

the tendency for groups to "favor" themselves by rewarding group members economically, socially, psychologically and emotionally in order to uplift one group over another.

54

ISLAMOPHOBIA

55

The fear or hatred of Muslims, Islam and related symbols.

55

ISM

A social phenomenon and psychological state where prejudice is accompanied by the power to systemically enact it.

56

JIM CODE

Coined by Ruha Benjamin, Jim Code identifies the range of discriminatory designs that encode inequity onto society by explicitly amplifying racial hierarchies and ignoring or replicating social divisions. In her book, **Race After Technology**, Benjamin argues that race itself is a kind of technology, designed to stratify and sanctify social injustice in the architecture of everyday life.

JOHN HENRYISM

John Henryism is a strategy for coping with prolonged exposure to stresses such as social discrimination by expending increasingly higher levels of effort which results in accumulating increasingly harmful physiological costs for the victim. Racial discrimination often forces African Americans to work harder than their white counterparts, which can lead to serious cardiovascular and physiological health issues.

GENERATIVE ADVERSARIAL NETWORKS (GANs) & CONVOLUTIONAL NEURAL NETWORKS (CNNs)

Generative Adversarial Networks and Convolutional Neural Networks are a class of machine learning that can be used to train neural networks to create deepfakes that fabricate increasingly deceptive articles of information (fake news), which is designed to confuse, manipulate, or inculcate innocent individuals. GANs and CNNs can go unnoticed and become increasingly devastating in perpetuity.

59

LOOKISM

Discrimination or prejudice based upon an individual's appearance.

60

MARGINALIZED

61

Excluded, ignored or relegated to the outer edge of a group, society, or community.

MEDICAL APARTHEID

Medical Apartheid is the systematic exploitation of African Americans and minorities by the medical system. It is the systematic experimentation, wrongful imprisonment, denial of proper services, and medical manipulation of African Americans in America. In her book, **Medical Apartheid**, Harriet A. Washington argues that "Diverse forms of racial discrimination have shaped both the relationship between white physicians and black patients and the attitude of the latter towards modern medicine in general." Today, Medical Apartheid has taken a technological turn, with implantable devices, Brain-Computer Interfaces (BCI), Electroencephalography, Deep Brain Stimulation (DBS), Transcranial Magnetic Stimulation (TMS), and Implantable Pulse Generators (IPGs) all of which are subject to hacking, falsification and illicit trafficking.

62

MICRO-INSULTS

Verbal and nonverbal communications that subtly convey rudeness and insensitivity and demean a person's racial heritage or identity. An example is an employee who asks a colleague of color how she got her job, implying she may have landed it through an affirmative action or quota system.

63

MICROINVALIDATION

Communications that subtly exclude, negate or nullify the thoughts, feelings or experiential reality of a person of color. For instance, white individuals often ask Asian-Americans where they were born, conveying the message that they are perpetual foreigners in their own land.

MICROAGGRESSIONS

65

Microaggression is a term used for brief and commonplace daily verbal or behavioral indignities, whether intentional or unintentional, that communicate hostile, derogatory, or negative attitudes toward stigmatized or culturally marginalized groups. Many marginalized groups report experiencing microaggressions in the workplace, job interviews, and everyday encounters. Harvard Professor Chester M Pierce, who coined the term, described microaggressions as "Assaults to black dignity and black hope [that] are incessant and cumulative...characterized by white put-downs, done in automatic, preconscious, or unconscious fashion."

MILITARIZATION (OF POLICE)

The militarization of police is the use of military equipment and tactics by law enforcement officers. This includes the use of armored personnel carriers (APCs), assault rifles, submachine guns, flashbang grenades, grenade launchers, sniper rifles, and Special Weapons and Tactics (SWAT) teams. The militarization of law enforcement is also associated with intelligence agency-style information gathering aimed at the public and political activists, and a more aggressive style of law enforcement. Criminal justice professor Peter Kraska has defined militarization of police as "the process whereby civilian police increasingly draw from, and pattern themselves around, the tenets of militarism and the military model."

NEGATIVE BAITING

Negative Baiting is a form of bullying. It is a provocative act used to solicit an angry, aggressive, or emotional response from another individual by focusing only on the negative elements of an interaction or encounter. It is one of the long-term stresses of dealing with toxic people in job interviews, the workplace, and other environments that should be supportive and healthy. For example, an interviewer may negatively bait a candidate by choosing to focus only on the seemingly negative elements of their work history or performance rather than taking an objective, constructive approach to the conversation.

NORMALIZATION

Normalization (sociology) or social normalization, is the process through which ideas and behaviors, like torture or racism, that fall outside of social norms come to be regarded as "normal." Many activists and medically targeted individuals describe their targeting as the "normalization of torture" given the consistent and casual manner in which it is inflicted. Coincidentally, Database Normalization is a statistical method of eliminating undesirable characteristics from a database or table of relations.

68

OPPRESSION

69

Results from the use of institutional power and privilege where one person or group benefits at the expense of another; oppression is the use of power and the effects of domination.

69

PREDICTIVE POLICING

Predictive policing is the usage of mathematical, predictive analytics, and other analytical techniques in law enforcement to identify potential criminal activity. Experts have pointed to the lack of transparency and biased training data used in predictive policing, which indicates that these tools are not fit for use. Such software is more accurate at predicting policing practices than it is at predicting crimes. In 2020, following protests against police brutality, a group of mathematicians published a letter in Notices of the American Mathematical Society urging colleagues to stop work on predictive policing. Over 1,500 other mathematicians joined the proposed boycott. Many activists report the repeated and unnecessary use of policing practices, sirens, and emergency service vehicles as a way for authorities to artificially bolster and trigger predictive policing algorithms and identifiers.

70

PREJUDICE

A preconceived judgment about a person or group of people,

usually indicating negative bias.

PROGRESS & RETRENCHMENT

This term refers to the pattern in which progress is made through the passage of legislation, court rulings and other formal mechanisms that aim to promote racial equality. Brown v. Board of Education and the Fair Housing Act are two prime examples of such progress. But retrenchment refers to the ways in which this progress is very often challenged, neutralized or undermined. In many cases after a measure is enacted that can be counted as progress, significant backlashes—retrenchment—develop in key public policy areas. Some examples include the gradual erosion of affirmative action programs, practices among real estate professionals that maintain segregated neighborhoods, and failure on the part of local governments to enforce equity oriented policies such as inclusionary zoning laws.

72

RACIAL GASLIGHTING

Racial gaslighting is a form of race-based psychological manipulation, intimidation, and emotional abuse that's seen in abusive relationships. It's the act of manipulating a person by forcing them to question their thoughts, memories, and the events occurring around them. The goal of gaslighting is to gradually undermine the victim's confidence in their own ability to distinguish truth from falsehood. Gaslighting is so prevalent in America that it has been recognized as a crime and health violation with very serious legal consequences. It is similar to trolling in that it can occur both online and offline and it is typically carried out by groups of people working together in a systematic and sinister manner.

73

RACIAL PROFILING

The use of race or ethnicity as grounds for suspecting someone of having committed an offense.

74

RACIST POLICIES

A racist policy is any measure that produces or sustains racial inequity between or among racial groups. Policies are written and unwritten laws, rules, procedures, processes, regulations and guidelines that govern people. There is no such thing as a nonracist or or race-neutral policy. Every policy in every institution in every community in every nation is producing or sustaining either racial inequity or equity between racial groups. Racist policies are also expressed through other terms such as "structural racism" or "systemic racism". Racism itself is institutional, structural, and systemic.

75

RE-FENCING (EXCEPTION-MAKING)

76

A cognitive process for protecting stereotypes by explaining any evidence/example to the contrary as an isolated exception.

RELATIONAL REPRESSION

Relational repression occurs when authorities work to separate, isolate, or ostracize individuals from friends, family, colleagues, and those they love in order to repress them or suppress their efforts. Chinese local officials frequently employ relational repression to demobilize protesters. When popular action occurs, they investigate activists' social ties and locate individuals who might be willing to help stop the protest. These members are then expected to use their personal influence to persuade relatives, friends, and fellow townspeople to stand down. Many activists report the use of lies, bribes, hacking, manipulation, entrapment, fake news, subterfuge, and coercion.

REPARATIONS

States have a legal duty to acknowledge and address widespread or systematic human rights violations, in cases where the state caused the violations or did not seriously try to prevent them. Reparations initiatives seek to address the harms caused by these violations. They can take the form of compensating for the losses suffered, which helps overcome some of the consequences of abuse. They can also be future oriented—providing rehabilitation and a better life to victims—and help to change the underlying causes of abuse. Reparations publicly affirm that victims are rights-holders entitled to redress.

78

RESILIENCE

79

The ability to recover from some shock or disturbance.

RESTORATIVE JUSTICE

Restorative Justice is a theory of justice that emphasizes repairing the harm caused by crime and conflict. It places decisions in the hands of those who have been most affected by wrongdoing, and gives equal concern to the victim, the offender, and the surrounding community. Restorative responses are meant to repair harm, heal broken relationships, and address the underlying reasons for the offense. Restorative Justice emphasizes individual and collective accountability. Crime and conflict generate opportunities to build community and increase grassroots power when restorative practices are employed.

80

REVERSO

Reverso is a form of bias and bullying wherein the culprit makes a conscious decision to view or misreport a situation the opposite of how it occurred in an attempt to reverse the outcome or evade blame. This includes the culprit falsely taking the role of the objective party in the conversation and assigning blame or subjectivity to the innocent party, thereby making themselves look innocent rather than guilty. Reverso can be viewed as a form of White Privilege wherein the offending party believes that they are always above reproach and have the power to decide blame independent of reality or facts. For example, an interviewer may ask a candidate a series of loaded questions and then receive a normal question from the candidate, but then say to the candidate, "well, that's a loaded question."

81

SAFE SPACE

82

Refers to an environment in which everyone feels comfortable expressing themselves and participating fully without fear of attack, ridicule or denial of experience.

82

SCAPEGOATING

The action of blaming an individual or group for something when, in reality, there is no one person or group responsible for the problem. It targets another person or group as responsible for problems in society because of that person's group identity.

83

SILENCING

The conscious or unconscious processes by which the voice or participation of particular social identities is excluded or inhibited.

84

SOCIAL IDENTITY

85

Involves the ways in which one characterizes oneself, the affinities one has with other people, the ways one has learned to behave in stereotyped social settings, the things one values in oneself and in the world, and the norms that one recognizes or accepts governing everyday behavior.

85

SOCIAL JUSTICE

Is both a process and a goal. The goal of social justice is full and equal participation of all groups in a society that is mutually shaped to meet their needs. Social justice includes a vision of society in which the distribution of resources is equitable and all members are physically and psychologically safe and secure.

SOCIAL SELF-ESTEEM

87

The degree of positive/negative evaluation an individual holds about their particular situation in regard to their social identities.

SOCIAL SELF-VIEW

An individual's perception about which social identity group(s) they belong.

88

STEREOTYPE

blanket beliefs, unconscious associations and expectations about members of certain groups that present an oversimplified opinion, prejudiced attitude or uncritical judgment. Stereotypes go beyond necessary and useful categorizations and generalizations in that they are typically negative, are based on little information and are highly generalized.

STINGRAY

An investigative technique used by both federal and local law enforcement in the United States to obtain information from cell phones by mimicking a cell phone tower. The devices which accomplish this are generically known as IMSI-catchers, but are commonly called Stingrays, a brand sold by the Harris Corporation. The United States Federal government has had access to stingray-type technology since at least 1995. In September 2015, the US Justice Department issued new guidelines requiring federal agents to obtain warrants before using stingray devices.

90

STRUCTURAL RACISM

A system in which public policies, institutional practices, cultural representations, and other norms work in various, often reinforcing ways to perpetuate racial group inequity. It identifies dimensions of our history and culture that have allowed privileges associated with "whiteness" and disadvantages associated with "color" to endure and adapt over time. Structural racism is not something that a few people or institutions choose to practice. Instead it has been a feature of the social, economic and political systems in which we all exist.

SUBVOCAL RECOGNITION

Subvocal recognition (SVR) is the process of taking subvocalization and converting the detected results to a digital output, aural or text-based. Developed by NASA, subvocal technology has been used against activists and protesters as a form of illegal eavesdropping and invasion of privacy. A person using the subvocal system thinks of phrases and talks to himself so quietly, it cannot be heard, but the tongue and vocal cords do receive speech signals from the brain, which can then be transmitted to the targeted party.

SYNTHETIC TELEPATHY

Synthetic Telepathy is created as the result of a (wire or wireless) Brain-to-Computer Interface (BCI) which can visualize and transmit the conscious and subconscious thoughts of an individual. Synthetic Telepathy was developed by the US Army in a $6.3million initiative to invent devices for telepathic communication. Research into synthetic telepathy using subvocalization is taking place at the University of California, Irvine. The first such communication took place in the 1960s using EEG to create Morse code using brain alpha waves.

93

SYSTEM OF OPPRESSION

94

Conscious and unconscious, nonrandom, and organized harassment, discrimination, exploitation, discrimination, prejudice and other forms of unequal treatment that impact different groups.

94

SYSTEMIC RACISM

95

In many ways "systemic racism" and "structural racism" are synonymous. If there is a difference between the terms, it can be said to exist in the fact that a structural racism analysis pays more attention to the historical, cultural and social psychological aspects of our currently racialized society.

95

TAIL-LIGHTING

Tail-lighting is a common practice among Venture Capitalists in Silicon Valley. Similar to a Police Officer pulling you over for a broken taillight, tail-lighting occurs when a VC obsessively points out very small or minute problems or differences in a diverse founder's startup in order to diminish their value or dignity vis-a-vis traditionally white founders. A big deal is made of something that is actually inconsequential. For example, a VC may disagree with a founder's view of a product's market size and therefore assume that the founder doesn't know what they're talking about despite their actual knowledge of the industry and supporting statistics. A common tail-lighting tactic is to elevate a very small difference of opinion into an accusation of an error or omission in an effort to impede a founder and their startup.

TARGETED INDIVIDUAL(S)

A Targeted Individual or Targeted Individuals (TIs) are people who are regularly and illegally harassed, tortured, mind controlled, gang-stalked, and/or spied upon by organized groups of persons.

TECHNOLOGICAL CASTE

The use of technology and infrastructure to reinforce and amplify racial hierarchies. Similar to the Indian Caste System, the Technological Caste System is designed to divide us and designate certain individuals or groups as "Untouchable" or "Unwanted." Divisions and hierarchies can hide in plain sight, appear rapidly, and persist indefinitely.

THE MEMORY MARKET

Coined by Cybersecurity company Kaspersky, *The Memory Market* is the underground market composed of the illicit trade in human memory, bio-resonance data, and medical data. Kaspersky and the US Department of Defence have identified illicit medical data and biohacking as one of the world's top threats to consumers and citizens. In 2013, Mount Sinai Hospital in New York City was found guilty of selling private patient health data in violation of HIPAA.

99

TOKENISM

Hiring or seeking to have representation such as a few women and/or racial or ethnic minority persons so as to appear inclusive while remaining mono-cultural.

100

100

TOLERANCE

Acceptance and open-mindedness to different practices, attitudes and cultures; does not necessarily connote agreement with the differences.

101

TRANSGRESSIVE

Challenging the accepted expectations and/or rules of the appropriateness of "polite society".

102

TRANSPHOBIA

The fear or hatred of persons perceived to be transgender and/or transsexual.

TRIGGERING / TRIGGER WARNING

Triggering is a form of intimidation, harassment, emotional abuse, and manipulation wherein culprits use and repeat keywords linked to stereotypes and rumors about an individual or group in an effort to scare them off an issue or subject. In so doing, a culprit is said to be issuing a "Trigger Warning" to the victim, which can often end with actual violence or physical abuse.

104

UNCONSCIOUS BIAS (IMPLICIT BIAS)

Social stereotypes about certain groups of people that individuals form outside their own conscious awareness. Everyone holds unconscious beliefs about various social and identity groups, and these biases stem from one's tendency to organize social worlds by categorizing. Occurs when someone consciously rejects stereotypes and supports anti-discrimination efforts but also holds negative associations in their mind unconsciously.

105

UNDOCUMENTED

A foreign-born person living in the United States without legal citizenship status.

106

UNDOCUMENTED STUDENT

School-aged immigrants who entered the United States without inspection/overstayed their visas and are present in the United States with or without their parents. They face unique legal uncertainties and limitations within the United States educational system.

V2K (VOICE-TO-SKULL)

V2K or Voice-To-Skull is another name for the microwave auditory effect (microwave hearing effect or the Frey effect). It consists of the human perception or infliction of audible clicks, or even speech, induced by pulsed or modulated radio frequencies. The communications are generated directly inside the human head without the need of any receiving electronic device. The effect has been reported by activists and targeted individuals as the result of auditory torture and targeting.

108

VETERAN STATUS

Whether or not an individual has served in a nation's armed forces (or other uniformed service).

VICTIM BLAMING

Victim blaming occurs when the victim of a crime or any wrongful act is held entirely or partially at fault for the harm that befell them. The study of victimology seeks to mitigate the prejudice against victims and the perception that victims are in any way responsible for the actions of offenders. Victim blaming can occur in a myriad of ways, both advertently and inadvertently.

110

WEAPONIZED RACISM

The adaption of racism, bias, and xenophobia, either biologically, technologically, or militarily, for its use as a weapon. A deadly form of racially encoded inequality that uses AI, social media, and biohacking to turn citizens against each other or limit the rights of certain individuals or groups. Many activists report the experience of "having an AI running against them."

111

WHITE FRAGILITY

Discomfort and defensiveness on the part of a white person when confronted by information about racial inequality and injustice.

112

WHITE PRIVILEGE

White Privilege is the spillover effect of racial prejudice and White institutional power. It means, for example, that a White person in the United States has privilege, simply because one is White. It means that as a member of the dominant group a White person has greater access or availability to resources because of being White. White privilege is the ability to grow up thinking that race doesn't matter. It is not having to daily think about skin color and the questions, looks, and hurdles that need to be overcome because of one's color. White Privilege may be less recognizable to some White people because of gender, age, sexual orientation, economic class or physical or mental ability, but it remains a reality because of one's membership in the White dominant group.

113

WHITE SUPREMACY

White supremacy is a historically based, institutionally perpetuated system of exploitation and oppression of continents, nations and individuals of color by white individuals and nations of the European continent for the purpose of maintaining and defending a system of wealth, power and privilege.

114

WOLDVIEW

The perspective through which individuals view the world; comprising their history, experiences, culture, family history, and other influences.

115

XENOPHOBIA

The fear or hatred of foreigners.

REFERENCES

1.   Benjamin, Ruha. Race After Technology: Abolitionist Tools for the New Jim Code. Wiley, 2019.

2.   Nick Couldry and Ulysses A. Mejias. The Costs of Connection: How Data Is Colonizing Human Life and Appropriating It for Capitalism. Stanford U Press, 2020.

3.   Maurianne Adams, Lee Anne Bell, Pat Griffin. "Glossary of Bias Terms." Washington University of St. Louis, edited by Maurianne Adams, Lee Anne Bell, Pat Griffin, Washington U of St. Louis, 25 Dec. 2020, students.wustl.edu/glossary-bias-terms/. Accessed 25 Dec. 2020.

4.   "Equity, Diversity and Inclusion Glossary of Terms" ["Equity, Diversity and Inclusion Glossary of Terms"]. Pacific U Oregon, edited by Pacific U Oregon, 25 Dec. 2020, www.pacificu.edu/life-pacific/support-safety/office-equity-diversity-inclusion/glossary-terms. Accessed 25 Dec. 2020.

5.   Washington, Harriet A. Medical Apartheid. Doubleday, 2006.

6.   Wikipedia. 2020.

7.   W.K. Kellogg Foundation, editor. "Racial Equity Resource Guide Glossary" ["Racial Equity Resource Guide Glossary"]. W.K. Kellogg Foundation, edited by W.K. Kellogg Foundation, 25 Dec. 2020, www.racialequityresourceguide.org/about/glossary. Accessed 25 Dec. 2020.

8.   Aspen Institute, editor. "11 Terms You Should Know to Better Understand Structural Racism" ["11 Terms You Should Know to Better Understand Structural Racism"]. Aspen Institute, edited by Aspen Institute, 25 Dec. 2020,www.aspeninstitute.org/blog-posts/structural-racism-definition/.Accessed 25 Dec. 2020.

9.   Racial Equity Tools, editor. "Glossary" ["Glossary"]. Racial Equity Tools, edited by Racial Equity Tools, 25 Dec. 2020, www.racialequitytools.org/glossary#decolonization. Accessed 25 Dec. 2020.

ABOUT THE AUTHOR

Champion Muthle aka Daniel Maree is an award-winning Writer/Director, Creative Strategist, Inventor, Philosopher, Creative Technologist, Afro-Futurist, and Social Entrepreneur. Alongside Malala Yousafzai, Champ is among the first group of Social Entrepreneurs in the world to be recognized by Forbes 30 Under 30. In 2012, the Pew Research Center celebrated Champ's work as the first and only campaign in history to surpass the Presidential Election in earned media. In 2013, the Mercury News recognized Champ as a 'Civil Rights Leader for the 21st Century.' Champ has worked on teams that have received McArthur Genius grants and his creative design work has been featured at the MoMA and the Library of Congress.

Prior to starting a globally recognized non-profit organization, The Million Hoodies Movement for Justice, Champ assisted the Social Impact team at Participant Media and led Digital Communications at the World Bank for the 2011 World Development Report on Conflict & Development. Later he spent over a decade in the creative industry as a VP of Digital Strategy, Innovation & Analytics where he received over a dozen creative awards including two Cannes Lions, two Art Director Awards, a Webby Award, and a Clio award. At 26, he was one of the youngest people and only African-American in history to receive two Cannes Lions.

Champ has been a contributing journalist and blogger for the Huffington Post, Global Voices, and TakePart.com. He has been profiled in numerous media outlets, including the New York Times, ABC World News, the Sydney Morning Herald, AdAge, and TheRoot. He has also been a guest lecturer at Columbia University, the UN Innovation Summit, the US State Department, Hamilton College, Summit Series, the Bill & Melinda Gates Foundation, South Philadelphia High School, Friend's Academy, and the French International School of New York. Champ holds 30+ patents and trademarks across multiple industries. He has a passion for screenwriting, sports, food, travel, and critical theory. He is a member of the Phi Sigma Tau Philosophy Honors Society and embraces Pragmatism, Liberation Theology, and Humanism.

In 2014 and again in 2017, Champ became the target of two multifaceted assassination attempts and a double deep fake reminiscent of COINTELPRO. He has chronicled his experience in his forthcoming memoir, This Little Light.